RACE CAR LEGENDS

CHELSEA HOUSE PUBLISHERS

RACE CAR LEGENDS

RUSTY WALLACE

Tara Baukus Mello

CHELSEA HOUSE PUBLISHERS
Philadelphia

Produced by Type Shoppe II Productions, Ltd.
Chestertown, Maryland

Picture research by Joseph W. Wagner

CHELSEA HOUSE PUBLISHERS

Editor in Chief: Stephen Reginald
Managing Editor: James Gallagher
Production Manager: Pamela Loos
Art Director: Sara Davis
Photo Editor: Judy L. Hasday
Senior Production Editor: Lisa Chippendale
Publishing Coordinator: James McAvoy
Cover Illustration: Keith Trego

Cover Photos: AP/Wide World Photos

First Printing

1 3 5 7 9 8 6 4 2

The Chelsea House Publishers World Wide Web site address is
http://www.chelseahouse.com

Library of Congress Cataloging-in-Publication Data

Mello, Tara Baukus.
    Rusty Wallace / Tara Baukus Mello.
        p.   cm. — (Race car legends)
    Includes bibliographical references and index.
    Summary: Examines the life, racing career, and future of
Rusty Wallace, who won the Winston Cup in 1989.
    ISBN 0-7910-5023-8 (hardcover)
    1. Wallace, Rusty, 1955 or 6- —Juvenile literature. 2.
Automobile racing drivers—United States—Biography—Juvenile
literature. [1. Wallace, Rusty, 1955 or 6- 2. Automobile racing
drivers.] I. Title. II. Series.
GV1032.W35M45 1998
796.72'092—dc21
[B]   98-25713
                                                                CIP
                                                                AC

CONTENTS

HOME AWAY FROM HOME

It had been three years and 86 races since Rusty Wallace won the pole position in a NASCAR Winston Cup Series event. The pole position is the number one starting position at the beginning of a race and is an important spot for any Winston Cup driver. Rusty won the pole for the 1997 Food City 500 by completing the fastest lap during the qualifying session. It meant that he would be first in line when the race started.

Only a fraction of a second separated Rusty from the driver who had placed fifth during the qualifying round. That driver was Jeff Gordon, who won the Food City 500 in 1995 and 1996. Also starting in the top five were Sterling Marlin, Ted Musgrave, and Rusty's younger brother, Kenny.

If Rusty won the race, he would receive the Unocal 76 Challenge bonus of $15,200, given to the winner if he also earns the pole position

Rusty Wallace in the crew garage prior to running pre-race test laps on the track at Daytona International Speedway, Daytona, Florida.

during the qualifying trials. The chances of Rusty winning this race, however, were small. Of the 72 events that had been run at the Bristol Motor Speedway, only 17 were won by the driver who started in the pole position. But that didn't worry Rusty Wallace.

"Ever since I won my first career Winston Cup race there back in 1986, Bristol has been like a home track for me. It really is a special place," said Rusty. After winning that first race at Bristol, Rusty won five more at the track, including the last race run there, the Goody's 500 the summer before. Rusty's six wins at Bristol ranked him third on the all-time win list for the track right behind Darrell Waltrip, who won 12 races, and Dale Earnhardt, who won at Bristol eight times.

Usually there are two chances to qualify for a Winston Cup Series event. But on Saturday, April 12, 1997, the second day of qualifying for the Food City 500, there was a steady rain falling on Bristol, Tennessee, and all chances for the drivers to better their times and improve their starting positions were literally and figuratively washed out. Because of a bad lap in the first qualifying round, Rusty's friend and seven-time NASCAR Winston Cup Champion Dale Earnhardt would start 29th out of 43 drivers.

The Bristol Motor Speedway is called "The World's Fastest Half-Mile" and is known for some of the most exciting races in NASCAR Winston Cup racing. Dale Earnhardt said, "Five hundred laps on this track takes its toll on you and your equipment. Keeping your car in one piece isn't always easy because everything happens so fast, you don't have any time to get out of the way." The track, a .533-mile oval, has banked concrete turns at a steep 36 degrees.

Because it rained on Saturday morning, the temperature in Bristol was about 15 degrees cooler on Sunday than it was on Friday when Rusty qualified for first. When drivers run their qualifying heats and practice laps before a race, the team uses that time to make adjustments to the car. Those adjustments are based on the conditions of the track, among

NASCAR driver Rusty Wallace prepares to don his helmet as he enters his #2 Ford on the starting grid for the Daytona 500 at the Daytona International Speedway February 15, 1998.

other things. A difference in temperature between when the car was adjusted in practice and the time of the race means the conditions of the track have changed and the car might not perform as well. But since the Bristol track was made of concrete instead of asphalt, the change in temperature didn't change the track conditions that radically. Rusty explained, "The asphalt, when it gets hot the car slows down and when it cools down, it speeds up."

When the Food City 500 started that Sunday, there were more drivers competing than ever before at the Bristol track. There were also more fans than ever before—almost 130,000—because the Speedway had been remodeled to include more seating. In fact, this was the largest group of fans ever to watch a sporting event in the state of Tennessee.

The race was filled with mishaps, and yellow caution flags were put out 20 times, tying an all-time NASCAR Winston Cup Series record first set during the Food City 500 in 1989. Although the day was filled with cars bumping and scraping each other, none of the drivers was seriously hurt. Dale Earnhardt was able to use a fender bender between Ernie Irvan and Bobby Labonte to his advantage. As the two cars came together, Dale was able to stay out of the way and pick up a lap he had lost earlier in the race.

But the most exciting part of the race was between Rusty and Jeff Gordon. Rusty led for 240 of the 500 laps during the three-and-a half-hour race. Jeff led the race on three different occasions for a total of 125 laps. During the last 100 laps, things started to heat up.

Rusty stole the lead from Jeff in lap 415, and by lap 437, he had gained a 1.34-second advantage. Then on lap 442, he lost that advantage. On the front stretch of the oval, Geoff Bodine knocked Jimmy Spencer into the wall. Geoff went into a spin and hit Steve Grissom in turn one. The caution flag went out, and Rusty lost his advantage. During the

Traveling at almost 200 mph, Rusty Wallace slides by the Pennzoil Grand Prix Pontiac on the inside of a turn at the Daytona International Speedway, Daytona, Florida.

Rusty Wallace is joined by his wife, Patti, in the winner's circle at Riverside International Raceway after winning the Budweiser 400, June 12, 1988.

caution, drivers must maintain their positions and drive as a group, each car equally spaced from the others.

The green flag was given on lap 451, and Rusty maintained the lead. After eight laps, he built another 1.28-second advantage over Jeff, but Jeff kept pressing and was soon on Rusty's bumper. Jeff's teammate, Terry Labonte, was able to close in on Rusty and Jeff. With only 15 laps left in the race, the three drivers were running bumper to bumper, and all of them wanted to win the race.

Jeff was the first one to make a move. Going into turn three on lap 486, Jeff stuck the nose of his Chevy under Rusty's rear bumper in an attempt to pass him. But Rusty held his ground. Three laps later, heading into the same turn, Jeff tried once more, but Rusty wouldn't let him get by. Terry Labonte, still in third, tried to pass Jeff twice, but Jeff wasn't about to give up his second-place slot.

In the final lap, all three drivers still fought to win the race. In turn three, Rusty and Jeff were close together. Jeff nudged Rusty, and he started to lose control of the car. He recovered, but not quickly enough. Jeff had passed him. Meanwhile, Terry saw what had happened and thought he could get by both of them to win the race. He gave it everything he had, but Jeff had scooted past Rusty fast and far enough to win. Rusty and Terry practically drag raced each other to the finish line, and Rusty barely placed second.

Jeff Gordon described the final lap this way: "I got a great run (on Rusty) and I kinda pushed him down the backstretch. We got into turn three, we touched, he got sideways, I jumped underneath the hole that he made. I'd never been in a shootout like that down to the finish, but I take my hat off to Rusty and Terry. They certainly raced hard."

Rusty wasn't surprised that Jeff hit him on the last lap. He said, "I probably would have done the same thing if I had gotten that close, going for the gold, for the checkers."

Going for the gold is what Rusty has done in his Winston Cup race car for more than 22 years. During that time he has won the 1989 Winston Cup Series championship and the 1991 IROC championship and has collected more than $14 million in winnings.

2
LEARNING THE ROPES

Rusty seemed to have a talent for racing from the start. His first race was an amateur stock car race at Lake Hill Speedway in Valley Park, Missouri, in a 1968 Chevelle given to him by his dad. The year was 1972, and one of the first people Rusty met racing was Winston Cup veteran Ken Schrader. Ken had just started racing the year before and had won the hobby championship, placing fourth in points. Ken remembers, "He [Rusty] didn't start at the start of the year because he had to wait until he was sixteen. He had better stuff, but I had a year's experience on him, and we were good friends—but it got tested pretty good, too."

Rusty's desire to continue racing grew as he raced regularly on local tracks in Missouri, Wisconsin, and Illinois. After working all day at a vacuum cleaner shop, he would spend

Rusty Wallace and his crew members celebrate their victory in the Splitfire Spark Plug 500 at Dover Downs, Delaware, September 19, 1993. Rusty came from behind to claim his second consecutive victory and the seventh of the season.

15

most of the night working on his race car with four or five guys who hung around the shop. From the beginning, long-time friend Don Miller was there helping him. Rusty, Don, and another friend named Charlie Chase shared the rent on a shop where they worked on their cars. Don, who had been in the business world for a while, knew that if Rusty was going to be a success, he would have to make racing his career. Now part owner of the team, Don told him, "You can keep doing that—weekend racing—and probably never go anywhere. To be successful at this thing, you're going to have to do it all the time, focus on what you're doing."

Rusty got serious after that advice from his friend. Don and he started by forming their own company which made frames for race cars, and they used the money they made to fund Rusty's career. Rusty became well known in the racing circuit throughout the Midwest over the next several years. In 1979 he won the United States Auto Club (USAC) stock car Rookie of the Year title, but 1980 was Rusty's big year.

Don Miller decided it was time for Rusty to compete in a race that would give him major recognition. The two decided that Rusty would go to Talladega Speedway in Talladega, Alabama, to run his USAC car in a Grand American race. Rusty took the car, which had previously been raced on dirt tracks, and modified the body for Grand American racing. Rusty had one of the fastest cars on the track, and on the last lap, he beat Ritchie Evans to the finish line and won the race.

His first Winston Cup race also took place in 1980. Don Miller approached Roger Penske

about supporting the team financially. Roger thought Rusty had what it takes to become a champion driver, but because Roger was reluctant, he agreed to back the team for only two races. Driving a Chevrolet Caprice at the Atlanta Motor Speedway, Rusty finished second to Dale Earnhardt in his first Winston Cup race. Although he didn't win, he impressed Roger Penske, who later became the team owner in 1991.

Driver Rusty Wallace discusses handling problems with his crew members during the first day of practice for the Daytona 500 at the Daytona International Speedway.

Rusty raced in several other Winston Cup races over the next few years, but his first opportunity to get in the big leagues full time came when owner Cliff Stewart asked Rusty to come on board to drive his Gatorade-sponsored Winston Cup car. Rusty had just won the American Speed Association (ASA) championship in 1983, and in December, after the big ASA awards banquet, he, his wife, Patti, and son, Greg, packed up and moved to North Carolina. Rusty raced for Cliff for the entire 1984 season. He competed in 30 races but didn't win any. In fact, things were a lot harder than Rusty had imagined they ever would be. "When I came down here and started racing them, it was a lot tougher, and I wasn't good at the politics part of it. I had never had to deal with that. I always called my own shots, built my own cars, made all the calls on race day from the car, when to pit and when not to pit, everything."

The first two years of Winston Cup racing were hard for Rusty. Although he never won a race, he learned what it took to race full-time on the most elite stock car tour in the world. In 1986, Rusty's career as a driver finally began to take off. He now worked for owner Raymond Beadle, and the entire team desperately wanted to win. Rusty won the fifth race of the season at Bristol Motor Speedway and again in Martinsville, Virginia. Although those were the only two races Rusty won that year, it established him on the Winston Cup circuit.

"You have to earn respect—entrance—into the circle of drivers, so to speak. After the first win, maybe they said I was lucky. After the second one, they couldn't say it was luck. That was a real important win," said Rusty.

Rusty's time with Raymond Beadle's team was successful. In 1989, he won the Winston Cup championship by winning six races and over two million dollars. In a few short years, Rusty went from rookie driver to one of the most talented drivers in Winston Cup racing history. Not only does Rusty have what it takes to win on the track, he is also a good businessman who knows how to motivate his crew. "I'm really big on organization, keeping the team organized," he said. "In fact, I almost get in fights with some of these guys sometimes because I know it's right." And Rusty really does know what's right. He has been learning about the technical aspects of race cars since he was a boy with his head under the hood of his father's cars. When he is not in the driver's seat, he's discussing some mechanical adjustment with one of the crew.

Many drivers believe that their role is simply to drive the car and that it's up to the crew to make sure the car is able to win. Rusty, however, goes into the shop and works on his car alongside his crew. It is this understanding of the mechanical side of racing that gives Rusty Wallace a competitive edge. Team owner Roger Penske said, "He would never be satisfied just to show up the next week with his helmet. He has to be in the shop, look under the car, be there when they start it up."

Rusty never stops learning, either. A few years ago, he didn't think computers could help his racing. At the time, the team was just beginning to work with computers, but they didn't depend on them. They relied on their own knowledge to make the adjustments they thought were right instead of allowing the computer to help them. "Now, I get right into it," Rusty said. "I don't know how to operate it, but I know how to turn it on. I go out, make a run, come back in and say, 'What does the computer say? Show me.' They show me and I'll say, 'Yeah, I could feel that,' or, maybe again, I didn't feel it."

It didn't take long for Rusty to decide he liked having the computer around. When the team started racing Ford Thunderbirds in 1994, they were having trouble getting the fuel distribution adjusted so it didn't damage the engine. It was the computer that helped them figure out the correct fuel distribution. Today,

Rusty Wallace gets a hug from Jimmy Maker of his pit crew after winning the Western 500 race at Riverside International Raceway, California. Crew members and their knowledge are an integral part of a winning NASCAR team.

computers are vital to the success of a Winston Cup team. Rusty's computer experts get feedback from the computer on nearly every aspect of the race car as it runs laps around the track. Every time Rusty makes a 10-lap run, the computer produces data that every member of the crew can use to make the car run better.

Perhaps it is Rusty's mechanical knowledge that makes him unafraid to drive his race car at 200 miles per hour around the track. "I don't think about dying in a race car. Honestly, I don't. I completely separate that. I can talk about it, easy. But I really feel my race car is one of the safest around, the way we do the roll cages, the way we do the seat belts, the seat installation. I feel really good about it."

3

ALL IN THE FAMILY

Like many race car drivers of today, Rusty grew up in a racing family. His dad, Russ, spent many a Saturday night on dirt and asphalt tracks, while Rusty's mom, Judy, watched from the grandstands. Once in a while, Judy found her way into the driver's seat. When she did, she won.

For Rusty and his younger brothers, Mike and Kenny, racing was as commonplace in the Wallace household as eating at the dinner table. When Rusty was three years old, he wrecked his first pedal car. He had a scooter when he was five years old whose tires he wore out trying to go fast. By age 10, Rusty was going all out in a go-kart. And his parents weren't surprised when he started driving a stock car and won his first race at 16 years of age. The Wallace family assumed that the three boys would race as a hobby but never thought one of the boys would make it a career.

Rusty Wallace finishes first, and his brother Kenny finishes second in the Bud Shootout at the Daytona International Speedway on February 8, 1998.

Racing was Rusty's first love. In fact, he did not care much about anything else, especially when he first got started.

Kenny, Rusty's younger brother who also races on the Winston Cup circuit, said that back then Rusty was in too big of a hurry. Kenny remembers one time when Rusty forgot about him. "They had run an ASA race at Fort Smith, Arkansas and we had a motor home and a race car hauler. We were in a restaurant eating and I had to go to the bathroom and they took off and left me. I walked out and nobody was there. I started to walk home and home was six hours away. Little did I know if I had kept walking I would have ended up in Florida, but I finally called home, crying, scared to death, and Mom and Dad contacted the Arkansas and Missouri state patrol and the cops ran down the motor home."

Although Kenny has never forgotten that incident, he hasn't had any trouble following in his big brother's footsteps. Kenny got his racing start in the ASA series just like Rusty and won the series' Rookie of the Year title in 1986. Three years later, Kenny went on to the NASCAR Busch Series, where he again won the Rookie of the Year title.

Kenny races the Square D Ford on the Winston Cup circuit and has competed in more than 100 Winston Cup races during his career. Although he has yet to post his first win, he has established himself as a driver with a promising future. In preparation for the start of his 100th Winston Cup race, Kenny said, "Winston Cup racing is very intense. Recently, I've learned what the level of intensity needs to be to race up front. Our whole team has stepped up to that [in 1997]."

The middle son of the Wallace family is Mike, who like his big brother, Rusty, began racing as soon as he was old enough to drive. Mike won more than 300 races on short tracks all over the Midwest, including the 1990 Mid-America Region champion of the Winston Racing Series. He first started racing in the NASCAR Winston Cup series in 1991 and went full-time in the series in 1994. Mike's career as a Winston Cup racer has not been easy since 1997 when he left LJ Racing after his Spam-sponsored car failed to make several races early in the year.

For the 1998 racing season, Mike drove the Purolator PureONE Filters Chevrolet in the NASCAR Craftsman Truck Series for team owner Kenny Schrader. Kenny knows that Mike really wants to be back on the Winston Cup circuit and that he may not be racing a SuperTruck in a year.

Little brother Kenny Wallace knows what it's like to be in a top-caliber Winston Cup car because he's been in the front pack more than once. Interestingly, Rusty has been there, too, and occasionally one can sense a bit of sibling rivalry. Kenny won his first pole for the 1997 Goody's Headache Powder 500 in Martinsville, Virginia. Kenny was 43rd out of 46 drivers to make the two-lap run to qualify for the race. He ran a lap of 20.153 seconds (93.961 miles per hour), placing him first in the pack of cars. Kenny's run was so good it almost broke the track record of 94.129 miles per hour, set by Ted Musgrave in 1994.

On race day, Kenny didn't lead any of the laps but fought hard to stay with the top contenders, including his brother Rusty, and finished sixth overall. Rusty finished fifth. There was a slight duel between the two brothers as they bumped into each other several times. Kenny said, "I didn't want to do it, but I had to. He [Rusty] makes people earn it when they pass him. I had to do it because it's racing, and I can't just let him by all the time. He earned his way by. He beat me in the left-rear about three or four times, which I loved. I loved every bit of it because it showed that we're putting all the potential we have into it. I was giving it everything I had."

Although Kenny and Mike live in the shadow of Rusty and his spectacular racing career, neither seems to mind. In fact, one time Kenny found himself right behind Rusty on the track, and it made him as happy as if he'd won the race himself.

It was February 8, 1998, at the Daytona International Speedway. The race was the Bud Shootout, a 25-lap sprint race that showcases the NASCAR Bud Pole Award winners of the prior year. On the last lap of the race, Kenny looked ahead of him and saw Rusty side by side with driver Jimmy Spencer. He knew that if he put his Square D Ford Taurus right behind Rusty's Miller Lite Ford Taurus, the two could work as a team by using the wind forces (drafting) to pull their two cars past Jimmy's and on to victory.

Drafting allows two cars to move much faster than one car, especially on superspeed-

Congratulated by ecstatic crew members, Rusty Wallace heads to the winners circle after winning the Bud Shootout.

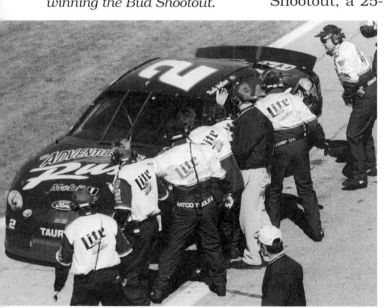

ways such as the Daytona International Speedway. Alone, Rusty's car had air come up over it and down onto the rear. The downward pressure on the rear end, combined with the air directly behind the car, caused the car to pull back slightly. But when Kenny ran up behind Rusty, he blocked most of the air behind the car, allowing his car to go as fast as Rusty's but without exerting as much force. As a result, Kenny was able to "push" Rusty, and the two cars moved together faster than if they had been traveling alone. In this way, Kenny ensured that both he and Rusty made it to the finish line first. And for the first time ever, the two brothers finished first and second.

"I made win who I wanted to win," said Kenny, "and I didn't want Jimmy to win— Rusty has helped me out in my career. So I pushed him the whole way. It was a big deal, it was a dream come true." Kenny went on to say, "Every year you look at the Labonte brothers and I tell you, it flat makes me jealous that they've done so many things together. All I wanted was to get in position to help my brother."

Jimmy Spencer said later: "You don't blame them, I mean, my God, if that was my brother I'd help him too. You can't begrudge any brother that. If my brother didn't, I'd never talk to him."

4

RACING RELATIONSHIPS

When Rusty first started racing, he was used to doing everything by himself. He was the one who made all the decisions from when to take pit stops to what adjustments to make on his race car. But Rusty also knew that if he wanted to make it in the big leagues—racing on the Winston Cup circuit—he would have to start depending on other people.

Cliff Stewart, a furniture manufacturer in High Point, North Carolina, called Rusty at the end of 1983 and asked him to drive his Winston Cup car sponsored by Gatorade. Cliff had owned NASCAR Winston Cup teams before and wanted to get involved in the sport again. He wanted Rusty in the driver's seat.

Cliff was a very demanding man, and it was not surprising that he and Rusty didn't get along very well. But Rusty was thankful that Cliff had given him the opportunity to race

Rusty Wallace running test laps in the 1996 Miller Lite Ford racer which was developed with partners Don Miller and Roger Penske over a number of seasons of NASCAR racing.

full-time in the Winston Cup events, and he wanted the team to win.

Throughout 1984 and 1985, Rusty raced for Cliff, although without much success. Rusty knew many of the other racers involved in Winston Cup racing—Neil Bonnett, Dale Earnhardt, and Darrell Waltrip—from his years of ASA racing, but for some reason, he just couldn't get the feel of Winston Cup racing. He had a hard time getting the car to handle well and wrecked it far too often. Everyone was surprised that the 1983 ASA champion wasn't performing better.

By the end of 1985, Rusty knew things weren't working out with Cliff, so he changed teams for the 1986 racing season. The new team owner was Raymond Beadle, and Blue Max sponsored his car.

Rusty found the satisfaction he was looking for with the Blue Max team. The crew was young and eager to win, the busy race shop was in a constant uproar, and the team barely made ends meet. But they won. A lot.

Five races into his first season with the Blue Max team, Rusty won his first race. It was at the track he now calls his home away from home: the Bristol Motor Speedway. He won again at Martinsville, Virginia. The Blue Max team was in all its glory when Rusty won the Winston Cup championship in 1989, after winning six races and bringing home over two million dollars that year alone.

After winning the championship, Rusty decided it was time to move on (he and Don Miller decided they were going to start a new team). Don was working for Roger Penske at the time, and he told his boss he was leaving

to go on the race circuit with Rusty. During this time, Roger Penske decided he wanted to get involved in NASCAR racing once again. Don said, "About October of '90, Roger said he was going to do it, and he said if we were going to do it, we were going to do it first-class or he didn't want to have any part of it." From that time, Rusty and Don became partners with

Rusty Wallace on his way to victory in the Budweiser 400 at the Riverside International Speedway in California on June 13, 1988.

Roger and remain partners today. "It's not like he reached in his pocket and gave us all this money and never wanted to see it again. We said, 'This is how we're going to pay it back to the company, and this is our company.'"

Today, the Penske Corporation is a billion-dollar company with more than 30,000 employees. Roger Penske is its chairman. Its divisions include Penske Truck Leasing, Detroit Diesel, Ilmor Engineering, Penske Auto Centers, and a bunch of Penske car dealerships. Penske Racing sponsors cars in both IndyCar and NASCAR. In addition, the company owns race tracks in Michigan, Pennsylvania, and California.

Rusty likes the fact that his team owner also owns several of the tracks on which he competes, although he's not sure if it gives him any advantage over the other race car drivers. In 1997, the California Speedway was scheduled to run its first NASCAR Winston Cup race, and Rusty was hoping he would have an advantage, especially after he used one of the seven testing sessions each driver gets every year at the track. Right before the June 1997 race, Rusty said, "We used one of our tests out there and I'm really glad we did. The set-up is different. The fastest line around the track is different. Sure, both of those tracks are two-mile ovals, but believe me you're out to lunch if you go out there thinking that what works at Michigan [another Penske-owned track] is what you'll need at California Speedway." Even though Rusty had a good track record of winning races in California, winning the inaugural California 500 wasn't in the cards. Rusty finished in 14th place.

Roger Penske has always taken an active role in the team. Once, after the Busch Clash in 1994, Rusty's team was allotted an hour of practice time. Initially, Rusty and the crew decided to cover the car up for the night and practice the following day. When Roger learned about this, he insisted that they use the practice time. "The whole team jumped on it. He [Roger] made them do it. We were ready to go home. He said, 'Get the car ready.' Now, we've got the shocks right, springs right and we've worked like blazes, and when he said we were going to do it, the whole team is like, 'Oh, shoot,'" said Rusty.

A recent development within Rusty's team was the purchase of 50 percent of the Michael Kranefuss-owned team by Penske South, which had Jeremy Mayfield, a new and still unproven young man, as its driver. In 1998, for the first time, Rusty had a teammate. At first, he wasn't thrilled with the idea, but he knew that the team was being stretched too thin and their chances of winning a championship weren't as good as he would have liked. By adding a second car, the team now had more crew members, equipment, and pooled knowledge without too much additional expense. Rusty explains: "I'll be the first to admit it, I wasn't crazy about another car in the garage. But this thing was put together with a lot of business sense. We didn't go out and hire a bunch of new people and new equipment. What we're doing is pooling resources. We can already see results."

For the first race of the 1998 season, the Daytona 500, Rusty and his new teammate, Jeremy, raced like they had been racing together for years. In the last 10 laps of the race, Jeremy found himself second in line. The young racer, who only started Winston Cup racing full-time in 1995, was sandwiched between Dale Earnhardt in the lead and teammate Rusty. Rusty and Jeremy were running so well that they planned to work together to pass Dale. They lost their opportunity in the last few laps of the race, however, when Rusty lost his place. Jeremy was holding strong until the final lap, when Bobby Labonte passed him. In the end, Jeremy finished third and Rusty crossed the finish line in fifth. Although it wasn't what they had hoped for, the new teammates were still happy. "We shoved him

A dazed Rusty Wallace is helped to a waiting ambulance after his car flipped over several times at the Talladega Speedway.

[Dale Earnhardt] and shoved him, but we couldn't get around him. Man, Jeremy's car and my car ran great all day long, so what a two-car team effort this was," Rusty said.

It wasn't the first time that Dale and Rusty had battled each other on the race track. In his first Winston Cup race, Rusty crossed the finish line second, right behind Dale. Although the two men have been friends for many years, sometimes on the race track that friendship becomes strained.

In 1993, in a race at the Talladega Speedway, Dale bumped into Rusty as he went into a turn, and Rusty lost control of his car. It flipped over several times, injuring him. Dale apologized to Rusty while he was recovering in the hospital, by taking all the blame for the accident. But Rusty remembered seeing Dale in his rearview mirror and pulling his car in front of him so Dale couldn't pass. He told Dale that he was partially to blame. When Rusty first started racing, he would not have been as likely to tell a fellow driver that he was partially at fault. But Rusty had learned a lot over the years, and most important, he'd learned how important relationships are, both on and off the track.

Reflecting on the Talladega accident, Rusty said, "Yeah, a lot of people said, 'You were too nice.' But pointing fingers doesn't gain anything. I learned in this sport a long time ago that getting on the radio, hollering and screaming, doesn't do anything."

THE CARS

Stock car racing officially began in 1947 when a group of drivers agreed to form an organization called the National Association of Stock Car Automobile Racing (NASCAR). It was headed by a man named Bill France. In the early days of NASCAR racing, the cars were almost completely stock, meaning that you could buy a car from a dealer and race it without making any modifications. In fact, many drivers drove their race cars to and from the track because they were the same vehicles they drove every day to and from work.

In the 1950s, no one thought much about the safety of the drivers. Often, drivers wore short-sleeved shirts, and seat belts weren't required in stock cars until 1953. By the early 1960s, NASCAR required that cars have changes to the basic stock models. Still, many stock cars had doors that opened and minimal

Driving a typical early stock car, "Fireball Roberts" wins the Firecracker 400 race at Daytona International Speedway, July 4, 1963. Both cars are Fords.

Robert L. Rewey, Ford's group vice-president in charge of their global motorsports program, with the new Taurus NASCAR Winston Cup car that replaced the Ford Thunderbird in the 1998 racing season.

roll cage systems. It wasn't until the 1970s that things really started to change.

During this time, factories that manufactured cars owned many NASCAR racing teams. The manufacturers thought that the fans bought the cars that were the fastest on the track on Sunday. As a result, manufacturers built race cars that looked similar to their stock models but could go a lot faster. Today,

stock cars are still loosely based on the show-
room models, such as the Chevrolet Monte
Carlo or the Ford Taurus, but there are many
differences, including body dimensions and
design of the engines.

Most Winston Cup teams have approxi-
mately 10 cars ready for racing at any time.
Teams need a different car for each type of
track, such as the superspeedways (i.e.,
Daytona), the intermediates (i.e., Charlotte,
North Carolina), the short tracks (i.e., Bristol,
Tennessee), and the road courses (i.e., Sears
Point, California). For each type of track,
teams usually have a primary race car and a
backup car, in case something goes wrong
with their first vehicle. Each car has certain
characteristics that make it more suitable for
a particular track. For example, a car built for
a superspeedway is designed to be more aero-
dynamically efficient. A road course car has
the weight balanced evenly on both sides so it
can turn easily to the left and right.

When Rusty teamed up with owner Roger
Penske, the team adopted the Penske tradition
of naming each car after it won its first race.
The tradition began on September 12, 1992,
when Rusty won at Richmond, Virginia, in his
first race with the new car. The car was named
Midnight because the race ended around
12:00 A.M. and the color of the car was midnight black. Midnight was a great car for
Rusty. He won 13 races and placed in the top
five in 31 of the 38 races he competed during
the 1993 and 1994 racing seasons. In 1993,
Midnight had a Pontiac body, but in 1994, the
body was removed and new sheet metal was
made to form a Ford body.

Rusty was driving Midnight in 1996 at the Charlotte Motor Speedway when he had an accident. He had started last in the Coca-Cola 600 and was working his way through the pack of cars when it happened. Rusty had advanced 36 spots when he got caught in a crash that wrecked both ends of the car. As far as everyone was concerned, Midnight was dead, and the car was placed in an out-of-the-way corner of the Penske race shop.

The following year, 1997, the guys on the crew decided to bring Midnight back to life in time for that year's race at Charlotte Motor

Mechanics and crew members make necessary adjustments to the Miller Lite Ford for an upcoming race in 1996.

Speedway. Dave Little, Penske Racing South's chief fabricator, said, "All the guys knew just how much the car meant to Rusty personally. We really took our time in making sure that this project was done with perfection. Instead of just sending the car outside the shop to have the front and rear clips put on, we put her on our jig here at the shop."

Although Midnight is the only car the team has brought back to life so far, there have been lots of cars that Rusty has named. Snake was named after Don "The Snake" Prudhomme, Rusty's good friend and owner of the Miller Lite NHRA Top Fuel drag racing team. After winning the first race on the Michigan Speedway, Rusty named his car Mannie after his uncle who died right before the win. And Killer had been a great road course car for Rusty after winning races at Sears Point, California, and Suzuka, Japan. This car earned its name because it "killed" the competition. "Killer" is also a word that Rusty uses to describe something that is the best.

Several cars won their first races at Richmond International Raceway, the same track where Midnight was named. In 1993, Midnight Rider was named there, and in 1995, a car named Ronnie was born. At another race at Richmond, Virginia, in 1996, Rusty felt pretty confident that he could win with his newest car, but the team placed a disappointing sixth. Rusty said, "When the race was over, there wasn't a smile on a single face around our transporter. Sixth-place was not what we came here for. It was 'disappointment city' and that's for sure. I told Robin [Pemberton, the crew chief] that we're not

Rusty Wallace contemplates strategy before the start of practice for the Jiffy Lube 300 in Loudon, New Hampshire.

using that car again until we find out what's wrong and fix it."

Robin Pemberton went to work on the car to try to figure out what was wrong. Eventually, Robin decided that there was a problem with the body, and the crew ended up replacing it. Rusty raced the car in March 1997 at Richmond, Virginia, in the Pontiac Excitement 400. This time he won. The car was named R.P. after its owner, Roger Penske. Rusty said that the name also could apply to his crew chief, Robin Pemberton.

No one on Rusty's crew really knows how any of his race cars will perform until he's competed in a race with it. The team, however, can get a good idea of a new car's potential during testing. NASCAR allows each team seven three-day tests at tracks the Winston Cup series uses during the race season. With a new car or at a new track, testing is crucial to figuring out how to set up the car to win.

When Rusty's team tested out the new track in Fort Worth, Texas, in 1997, the entire crew was hard at work: a total of nine crew members were out on the track watching Rusty. Rusty said, "For the first couple of hours, we focused on the lines around the race track. We had Robin down in Turns 3 and 4 analyzing our lines and corner speeds versus all the other guys. Then he moved down to Turns 1 and 2 for an hour or so. We had guys on pit road, guys on the truck. . . . We were getting feedback from every direction. We had George [Whitley, team engineer] and Tom Hoke [shock specialist] and all the computers churning out data. We even had our team pilot [Captain Bill Brooks] up in a suite reading off the other cars' lap times and keeping scope on the whole track."

It's not certain if all this testing actually helps a team win a race or not, but without it the team wouldn't keep learning about its cars, about the track, and about how to win. In order to win, a team has to keep on the edge and learn everything it can.

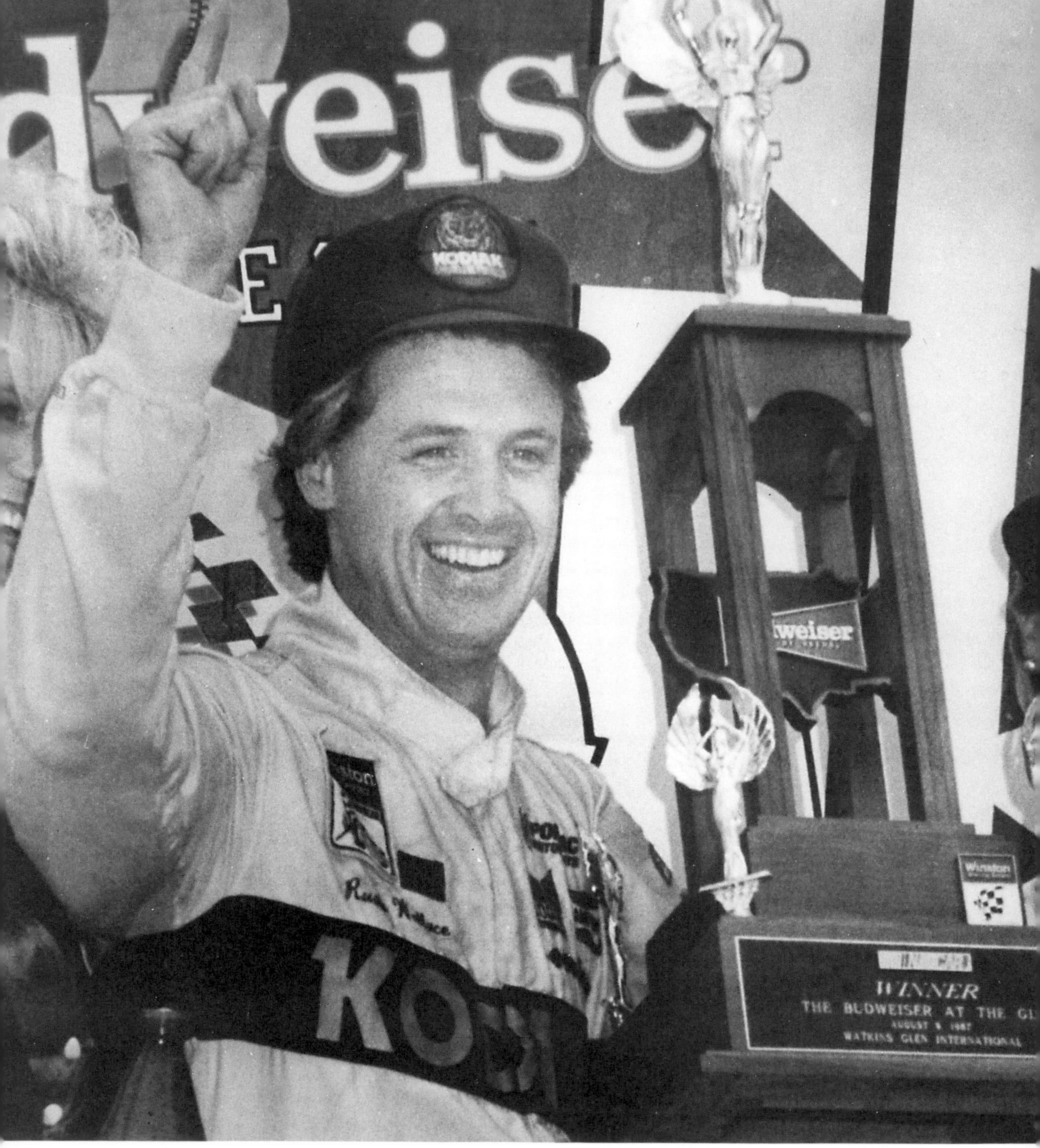
WINNER
THE BUDWEISER AT THE
WATKINS GLEN INTERNATIONAL

NUMBER ONE

Rusty Wallace likes being number one. Although everyone wants to win at whatever sport he or she plays, Rusty is a bit different. Not only does he like to win, he also likes to be the first person to try something different with his race car or to win the first time a new race is run.

In 1996, Rusty's team began working with Rockwell Space Systems and the National Aeronautics and Space Administration (NASA) to test special insulation materials that were designed to reduce the heat in the driver's compartment of NASCAR Winston Cup cars. Workers at the Kennedy Space Center in Cape Canaveral, Florida, took the same thermal blanket material that was used in the space shuttle and applied it to Rusty's car. The idea was that the special insulation would lower the temperature inside the car.

Rusty Wallace reacts in the winner's circle after winning the Budweiser at the Glenn NASCAR race at Watkins Glenn International Speedway, August 10, 1987.

Rusty said, "The cooler you keep the car, the better concentration the drivers will have and I think you'll see safer racing. The whole thing is to cool everything down and when you cool everything down that's just going to bring the driver's performance way up."

Once the insulation was installed, the team took the car down to the Daytona International Speedway for testing. Rusty made an extended run with the insulation while the computer

Rusty Wallace shows off the Thunder Special 100 trophy after winning the NASCAR exhibition race at the Suzuka Circuit, central Japan, November 24, 1996.

measured the temperature in various parts of the car. For the second part of the test, the team removed the insulation and Rusty made another run. The team discovered that the insulation cooled the driver's compartment by between 30 and 50 degrees. In the hottest part of the car, near the driver's feet where the exhaust collector comes through the left tailpipe, it reduced the temperature of the floorboard by 150 degrees. Although the test was a success, it was up to NASCAR to decide if and how the material is to be used during a race.

For Rusty, being first isn't limited to just testing. Rusty has an amazing record of winning inaugural races. In 1993, the New Hampshire International Speedway opened in Loudon, New Hampshire. The 1.058-mile track is relatively flat, with only 12 degrees of banking in the turns. During the first Jiffy Lube 300, Rusty started in 33rd position and amazingly worked his way through the field of cars to win the race.

A few years later, NASCAR made history by holding an exhibition race in Suzuka City, Japan. The track is a complicated road course 1.4 miles long and includes first-gear hairpin turns, sixth-gear straightaways, and everything in between. Thirty drivers from the United States are invited to compete each year.

In the first NASCAR Suzuka Thunder Special 100 in 1996, Rusty hoped he could make racing history. "We're going into this race focused on bringing the winner's trophy back home. This is a new deal, NASCAR racing going overseas, it's history-making and we want to be the headline story connected with it."

Rusty and Dale Earnhardt had been to Suzuka City earlier in the year for a test and a promotional tour. Although Rusty had driven on the track during testing, he didn't feel that gave him an advantage over the other drivers competing. He said, "When we went over there for the test, we used a car that was more or less a show car. This time we're going back with a bonafide winning road course car. If we have any advantage at all, it'll be that we know how to get through the airports on the way there."

The Suzuka City race is unusual in many aspects. The race is held rain or shine, and as a result, each car was equipped with windshield wipers and brake lights for the first time. Goodyear even supplied special tires for rain, to which teams switch in the event of bad weather. Qualifying trials and the running of the race itself are also unusual. Drivers qualify by completing two laps separated by a two-tire pit stop. During the race, drivers run 50 laps and take a 10-minute intermission so that the top 10 drivers are inverted for the final 50 laps.

This first race in Japan was so different from the other races that it made Rusty want to win it even more. Crew chief Robin Pemberton said, "Rusty will be ready to win over there . . . whether it's on the race track or to see who can get to the hotel first or to see who gets the front compartment of the roller-coaster outside the race track. [An amusement park is located next to the race track.] I look for it to be in typical Rusty-fashion all the time we're in Japan. We'll strive to be the first, and best, in everything we do."

Rusty was off to a good start when he hit the race track in Japan. During qualifying, he recorded the best lap time and got the pole position for race day. When the race started, Rusty led the way for the first 38 laps. On lap 39, Rusty's brakes began to heat up, and Jeff Gordon was able to pass him and take the lead. Determined to stay in the race, Rusty dropped back a bit, letting off on the gas pedal early in the turns so he didn't have to use his brakes as much. By the time the first 50 laps were finished, Rusty was in eighth place. During the 10-minute intermission between

Rusty Wallace on the track, running test laps to get the new Ford Taurus ready for the 1998 Bud Shootout.

the first and second segments, the top 10 cars were inverted, leaving Rusty to start the second half of the race in third position. At the start of the second half, Terry Labonte passed Johnny Benson to take the lead and Rusty got stuck behind Johnny. By lap 55, Rusty passed Terry and took the lead. He kept the lead while behind him, Dale Earnhardt and Jeff Gordon closed in. But neither man was able to get by Rusty, who won the race with a 1.192-second lead over second-place finisher Dale Earnhardt.

Everyone knew how badly Rusty wanted to win this race, and to say that he was happy is an understatement. Rusty said, "It's one [win] that we'll all remember forever. It's history and we're the first team to win over here. It's probably something all of our kids and grandkids will remember. It's about the neatest deal that's happened to me and the guys in a long, long time, I'll tell you that." The team celebrated the victory by stopping off for a few games at a local bowling alley before the bus came to take the crew members to the airport.

The 1998 season started off well for Rusty and the team, who had spent the winter testing the new Ford Taurus. Ford Motor Company switched from Thunderbird to Taurus bodies for the 1998 racing season, and Rusty's team was key

Rusty Wallace, winner of 47 NASCAR races as of the beginning of the 1998 season.

in helping Ford test the bodies. In the first race of the season, the Bud Shootout, Rusty made history again, this time by winning the race and the first victory for the Taurus. The 25-lap race, reserved for the Bud Pole Award winners from the previous year, was filled with controversy.

Jeff Gordon was leading the race when Ward Burton crashed on lap 23. The caution flag came out. Because laps under caution don't count in this race, the cars were lined up for a restart for the last two laps. On lap 24, Jeff was still in the lead when Bobby Labonte, John Andretti, and Joe Nemechek got tangled together and another caution flag came out. This time the cars were lined up two-by-two for the restart with Jeff on the inside and Rusty on the outside leading the pack. At the restart, Rusty jumped ahead of Jeff. Jimmy Spencer was right next to him when Rusty looked in his rearview mirror and saw his brother Kenny coming up behind him. Kenny created a draft that gave Rusty the extra push he needed to finish first. Rusty remarked, "I was hoping he would help me because he is my brother, right? Well, he got behind me and when he did that my car took off like a bullet."

After the race was over, Jeff Gordon complained about what happened in the last lap. He said that Rusty had started too soon. "I'm really disappointed NASCAR let the restart get away like that," Jeff said. "Rusty just jumped the start. They say we're supposed to restart when we get to the orange 76 ball, but Rusty started way before that." Jeff, who was driving at caution speeds when Rusty passed him, also had broken the fourth gear in his car.

NASCAR officials said that Jeff didn't understand where the race was supposed to restart. They said that the race didn't restart at the orange 76 ball but where the track meets pit road and the corner of the grass. A white line is painted on this spot. NASCAR spokesman Jeff Motley said, "We also say that cars must maintain their speed leading up to the restart.

Rusty Wallace waits while his pit crew changes tires on his race car during a pit stop at the running of a practice session at the Daytona International Speedway.

At the point where the restart was to take place, the No. 24 car [Jeff Gordon] had slowed down and the No. 2 car [Rusty] maintained his speed. How do you penalize the No. 2 for maintaining his speed?"

Rusty was just doing what he knows how to do best: he went for the win. "When I got there [at the restart spot], I hit it. In these shoot outs, you don't wait around to see what someone else is going to do."

LIFE OFF THE TRACK

Rusty's whole life centers on racing. It is his career, his business, and his love. It also takes up most of his time. Rusty's typical week starts at the race shop on Tuesday. There, he meets with the crew. They discuss problems that arose during the previous week's race and figure out the strategy for the next race. Wednesdays are spent planning the week and organizing the business. Rusty might talk over scheduling with his pilot or check in at one of his car dealerships. On Thursdays, he's back at the race shop to check on the final details before the team heads out to the next race. Fridays, Saturdays, and Sundays are spent at the track practicing, qualifying, and finally, racing. Depending on how far away the race is, Rusty either drives his motor home or flies to the races in his personal airplane.

Rusty Wallace taking a break between test laps being run prior to the Daytona 500 at the Daytona International Speedway.

By Sunday night, Rusty is usually back home with his wife, Patti, and three children, Greg, Katie, and Stephen, to spend some quality time with his family. "Sunday night after a race I get home and the first thing I do is turn the answering machine off. It seems everybody wants to call and bug you on Sunday night. I'll take a shower, really get to feeling good, get a little something to eat and get down there and play with the kids a little and talk to Patti. And I don't want to be interrupted by the outside world."

Mondays, too, are reserved for his family, although there are usually problems or decisions to be made that pull him away. When one is a top-notch race car driver, there's always a publicity appearance or a charity function that must be attended. For the most part, Rusty works on some aspect of his racing business six days a week, up to 12 hours a day.

And even when Rusty has free time, he still likes to go fast. Whether in airplanes, motorcycles, boats, or hot rods, Rusty likes his toys to be able to get going in a hurry. No matter what mood he's in, he's got a toy for it. If he feels like getting the wind in his hair, he takes a ride on his motorcycle. If he's in the mood for the rumble of an engine, he takes his hot rod out for a drive. Lazy days, although there are only a few, are spent puttering around on the family's boat on a lake near their home.

Rusty's favorite pastime is flying. He loves the peacefulness of soaring above the world and often pilots his own plane to the races. Although he's almost as knowledgeable about flying as he is about racing, he sometimes winds up in trouble.

In 1997, Rusty decided to fly his plane from Concord, North Carolina, to Darlington, South Carolina, to practice for the TranSouth Financial 400. He had his brother Mike and Mike's daughter, Chrissie, with him. When the three arrived at the airport in Concord, there was dense fog. They had waited about an hour when Rusty decided to take off. He figured the fog would burn off as it had so many times before. "I had six hours of fuel on board so I figured I had no problems. I flew over here and it

Front view of the sleek, streamlined Ford Taurus especially prepared for the 1998 racing season.

wouldn't clear up! I kept holding and holding and finally it got to 10 o'clock. I was afraid I was going to miss practice." Rusty had to come up with a plan quickly. He flew to Fayetteville, North Carolina, nearly 95 miles from Darlington and the closest town clear of the fog, and drove from there to Darlington. By the time they arrived, he and Mike had only missed about 25 minutes of practice.

Frequently, Rusty takes his family with him to the races. During his downtime at the track, the family spends time together in their motor home. Rusty and Patti knew each other for a long time before they got married. Their families, who were both involved in racing, met at the Lake Hill Speedway in St. Louis, Missouri. In 1980, on Rusty's birthday, he and Patti got married. Their youngest son,

Rusty Wallace today: What's next?

Stephen, who was 10 years old in 1998, loves racing and is fearless like his dad. He's been go-karting since he was five years old.

Despite his efforts to keep his life "normal," Rusty Wallace takes part in some unusual activities. Prior to the Save Mart 300 in Sears Point, California, in 1996, Rusty spent a day as a taxi cab driver for a special publicity event for journalists and television reporters. He drove a real taxi cab through the streets of San Francisco with area journalists as his passengers. He drove them down famous Lombard Street, the most crooked street in the world, and showed off some unique driving skills like driving on the sidewalk. In a publicity event in 1998, this time for the first Las Vegas 400 at the new track in Las Vegas, Rusty shot a commercial with an Elvis impersonator in the passenger seat. Billboards all over the city talked about the "Adventures of Rusty."

Although that event was just a publicity stunt, Rusty's life really has been one big adventure. Rusty's fans are waiting to see what his next adventure will be.

CHRONOLOGY

1956   Rusty Wallace is born on August 14 in St. Louis, Missouri.

1966   Rusty starts go-kart racing.

1972   Rusty wins his first amateur stock car race.

1979   Rusty is named USAC Rookie of the Year.

1980   Rusty competes in his first Winston Cup race at the Atlanta Motor Speedway. He places second to Dale Earnhardt.

1983   Rusty wins the ASA championship.

1984   Rusty begins Winston Cup racing full-time for owner Cliff Stewart.

1986   Rusty begins driving the Blue Max-sponsored car for Raymond Beadle.

1989   Rusty wins the Winston Cup championship.

1991   Rusty teams up with the Miller Brewing Company and team owner Roger Penske.

1992   Rusty begins the tradition of naming his cars after they win their first race. Midnight is christened.

1993   Rusty wins the inaugural Jiffy Lube 300 at the New Hampshire International Speedway.

1996   Rusty wins the inaugural NASCAR Suzuka Thunder Special 100 in Suzuka City, Japan.

1998   Rusty wins the Bud Shootout, the first win ever for the new Ford Taurus body.

STATISTICS

YEAR	RACES	WINS	TOP 5	TOP 10	WINNINGS
1980	2	0	1	1	$22,760
1981	4	0	0	1	12,895
1982	3	0	0	0	7,655
1983	0	0	0	0	1,100
1984	30	0	2	4	195,927
1985	28	0	2	8	233,670
1986	29	2	4	16	557,354
1987	29	2	9	16	690,652
1988	29	6	19	23	1,411,567
1989	29	6	13	20	2,247,950 *
1990	29	2	9	16	954,129
1991	29	2	9	14	502,073
1992	29	1	5	12	657,925
1993	30	10	19	21	1,702,154
1994	31	8	17	20	1,914,072
1995	31	2	15	19	1,642,837
1996	31	5	8	18	1,665,314
1997	32	1	8	12	1,505,260
CAREER	428	47	140	225	$15,925,295

Won Winston Cup championship

FURTHER READING

Burt, Bill, *Behind The Scenes of NASCAR Racing*. Osceola, Wisconsin: Motorbooks International, 1997.

Huff, Richard, *Behind The Wall: New Edition Captures Terry Labonte's 1996 NASCAR Season*. Chicago: Bonus Books, 1997.

Huff, Richard, *The Insider's Guide To Stock Car Racing*. Chicago: Bonus Books, 1997.

Olney, Ross R., *How To Understand Auto Racing*. New York: Lothrop, Lee & Shepard Books, 1979.

Martin, Gerald, *Rusty Wallace, Racer*. Tucson, Arizona: AZTEX Corporation, 1994.

ABOUT THE AUTHOR

Tara Baukus Mello is a freelance writer who specializes in the automotive industry. She has published over 1000 articles in newspapers and magazines. Baukus Mello is also the author of *The Pit Crew*, part of the Race Car Legends series. A graduate of Harvard University, she lives in southern California, where she cruises the streets in her 1932 Ford pickup street rod with her husband, Jeff.

INDEX